DIGITAL ART

DIGITAL ART

A COMPLETE GUIDE TO MAKING YOUR OWN COMPUTER ARTWORKS

David Cousens

ARCTURUS

Picture credits:
All images by David Cousens, apart from the following: page 33 (bottom), Richard Rosenman;
page 44 (top), Corbis; page 48 (top left), illustration by Tim Shelbourne; pages 48–51, photo by
Tigz Rice (model, Coco Dubois). Gorilla image (page 40) appears courtesy of Digital Arts magazine.

Front cover: All images by David Cousens.

Note for Mac users:
The instructions in this book are given for Windows. The following conversions apply for Mac users:

Windows	Mac
Alt	Option
Crtl	Command
Right-click	Ctrl-click

This edition first published in 2014 by Arcturus Publishing Limited

Distributed by Black Rabbit Books
P.O. Box 3263
Mankato
Minnesota MN 56002

Copyright © 2014 Arcturus Holdings Limited

Library of Congress Cataloging-in-Publication Data

Cousens, David.
 Digital art : a complete guide to making your own computer artworks /
David Cousens.
    pages cm. -- (Creative workshop)
 Includes index.
 Summary: "Instructs readers in techniques for using digital art
programs"--Provided by publisher.
 ISBN 978-1-78212-410-8 (library binding)
1. Digital art--Technique--Juvenile literature. I. Title.
N7433.8.C685 2014
776--dc23
                         2013004693

Printed in the USA

SL003588US
Supplier 02, Date 0114, Print Run 3388

Contents

Chapter One
Setting Up

This chapter eases you into the world of digital art. It explains some of the terminology you will encounter, looks at the most commonly used tools, and guides you through the choices you will be presented with when you first start out.

RGB, CMYK, and DPI

When you create a new file you are presented with a number of choices about the options available. This can be a bit confusing for the uninitiated. Here is a beginner's guide to the various technical terms.

What is the difference between RGB and CMYK?

RGB (red, green, blue) and CMYK (cyan, magenta, yellow, and key, or black) are the two main color options available when you create a file. For screens and monitors emitting light, RGB is the most accurate way to display colors. CMYK is the best choice for physical formats, as printed pages absorb light.

So which color mode should you choose?

For RGB files, programs such as Photoshop have a lot more available options (including filters, layer styles, and adjustment layers). It is therefore best to use this color mode when painting. If you need to print an artwork, you can convert the file from RGB to CMYK when the image is finished.

Size matters!

DPI/PPI refers to the number of dots/pixels per inch—the density of dots in the image when it is reproduced either physically (printed on paper) or displayed on a monitor.

The native resolution of a computer screen is 72 DPI, which is the usual size for displaying an image on the internet. However, to ensure high quality you should print your artwork at a minimum of 300 DPI.

So what size resolution should you choose?

As a rule, it's best to work on a document at 300 DPI, if you want to avoid problems when printing your work at a later date. You can always scale artwork down for the internet, but scaling digital artwork up may result in a loss of quality and increased pixelation.

Workspaces

Although every new version of Photoshop looks slightly different, the overall layout of the workspace remains the same. Here's how to find your way around it.

What's on screen?

The *Menu Bar* is located at the top of the screen, giving access to the majority of Photoshop's functions.

The *Options Bar* is located immediately beneath the *Menu Bar*. Here you will find options you can modify, depending on the tool you have selected at the time.

The *Toolbox* is on the far left of the workspace and contains a number of icons for tools. The tools are collected into groups that perform a similar function—for example, selection, painting and editing, path and shape, and so on.

Most of the screen space is allocated to the document window (the area where you paint).

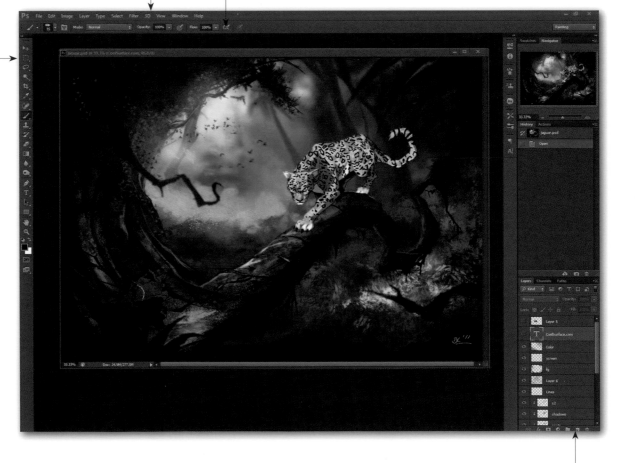

On the far right is the *Panel Dock*, which gives you an editable selection of panels. These include the "History" palette and access to layers, channels, colors, and swatches.

In Photoshop CS5 and CS6, you have the option of automatically assigning a workspace. For example, you can choose a workspace for painting or for 3D and Photoshop will offer you the relevant tools for your task.

For Photoshop users, Corel Painter 12 features an instantly familiar workspace, with the main toolbar and palettes located in the same positions as for Photoshop. Painter 12 features an option to apply alternative workspaces created by artists for specific methods of drawing, such as a concept sketching and illustration. There is also a creativity workspace for generating ideas quickly.

Autodesk Sketchbook Pro features a more open workspace than Photoshop and Painter 12. A dock at the bottom left gives access to tools. There are fewer tools available in this program than in others, but Sketchbook allows you to edit your work to perfection.

Pixels and Vectors

There are two ways of working digitally—with pixels or with vectors.

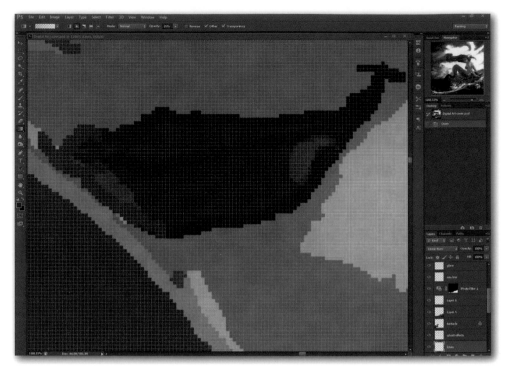

Pixel-based artwork

Pixel-based (or pixel-element-based) artwork (also referred to as raster or bitmap graphics) is made up of a large grid of tiny squares. Each square is assigned a color. The colored squares are used to build up an image that looks like flat color when viewed from a distance.

Pixel images are great for painting and photography as they can be used with ease to achieve a wide range of tonal variation. Although a pixel image can be scaled down successfully, the quality is impaired if you attempt to increase its size. Pixel images are favored by programs such as Adobe Photoshop, Corel Painter, and Autodesk Sketchbook Pro. These programs typically aim to replicate a traditional style of working. If used with a pen stylus, the result is very similar to drawing or painting.

Vector-based artwork

Vector-based artwork differs from pixel-based artwork to the extent that it relies on mathematical algorithms to determine the shape and size of all lines drawn. Vector graphics are ideally suited to logo design and typography, as they can be scaled infinitely and remain crisp, no matter how large you make them, or how closely you zoom in. Vector-based programs are best used in conjunction with the *Pen Tool*. Manipulation of the *Pen Tool* can take a bit of getting used to, but it offers great control and precision.

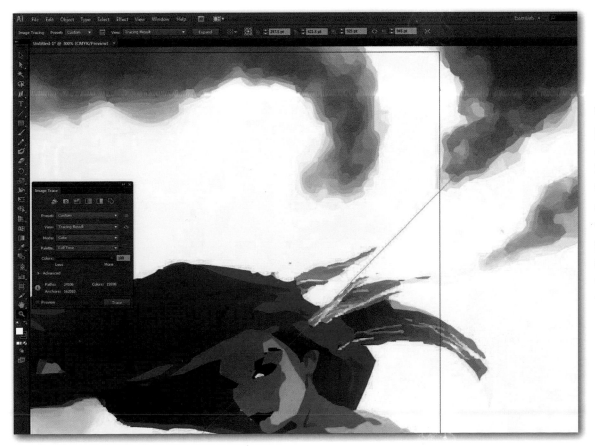

Vectors are used in programs such as Adobe Illustrator, Flash, and certain tablet-based drawing apps. However, vector-based artwork programs are not suitable for images with large areas of tonal detail.

Basic Noncreative Tools

These Photoshop tools are good for assisting with creative tasks, but aren't used for creative purposes on their own.

△ Using the *Rectangular Marquee Tool*

The *Move Tool*

The *Move Tool* is used to manipulate elements of the image. Holding down the Shift key before using the *Move Tool* constrains movement to horizontal or vertical straight lines; holding down the Alt key before using the *Move Tool* duplicates the layer.

With the *Move Tool* selected, you can use the arrow keys to nudge things one pixel at a time. Right clicking with the *Move Tool* gives you a list of layers with a pixel on them beneath the current location.

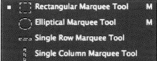

The *Marquee Tools*

The *Marquee Tools* allow you to make a selection from a predefined shape, for example, a rectangle, an ellipse, a single row, or a single column. They can be set to create a new selection with each mouse click. Alternatively, you can set the *Marquee Tools* to add or subtract from selections and to intersect with them. All selections can have their margins feathered (blurred) to give a soft-edged effect.

The *Lasso Tools*

The *Lasso Tool* allows you to trace out selections. There are three types of lasso. The freehand *Lasso Tool* is used to manually trace the areas for selection. The *Polygonal Lasso Tool* makes a selection of multiple points in straight lines.

▷ The *Magnetic Lasso Tool* guesses the pixels you want to select and snaps to the edges of an object by measuring the contrast of the neighboring pixels. If the colors you are working with are very similar, you can alter the levels of tolerance in the *Options Bar*.

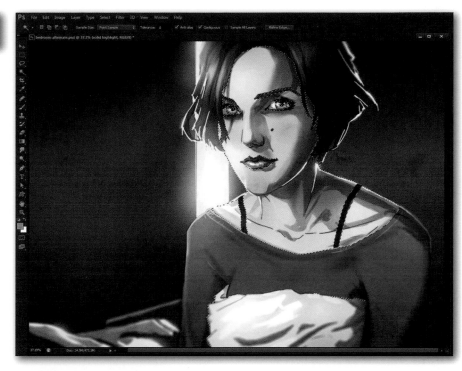

The *Magic Wand Tool*

The *Magic Wand Tool* works a little differently from the other selection tools. It makes selections based on the color you click on. With a low tolerance setting, the *Magic Wand Tool* will only select colors close to the first color you click on; to select a broader range of similar colors, simply use a higher tolerance setting.

The *Quick Selection Tool*

The *Quick Selection Tool* (added in Photoshop CS3) is a more advanced version of the *Magic Wand Tool.* It lets you paint your selection with a brush; you can change the size of the brush as and when you need to.

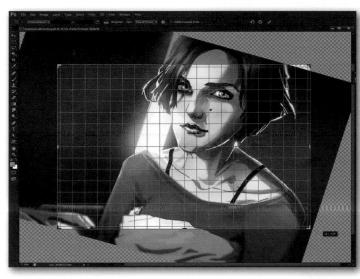

The *Crop Tool*

The *Crop Tool* has a number of useful functions beyond simply cropping unwanted areas from an image. You can rotate an image as you crop it by releasing the mouse button and dragging one of the corners of the marquee.

With the *Perspective Crop Tool* you can correct any distorted perspectives in an image by dragging the handles manually to match the areas you want straightened.

You can also set the *Crop Tool* to hide the cropped area instead of permanently deleting the pixels.

You can automatically crop different images to one specific size by selecting your active image and clicking on the "Front Image" button in the *Options Bar*. Now, when you use the *Crop Tool* on another image, it will automatically match the size of your original image.

The *Crop Tool* doesn't just reduce the size of images. If you drag the handles beyond the boundary of your canvas, you will increase the size of your document.

Color Selection

There are several ways to select color.

Clicking on one of the two color squares in the bottom of the *Toolbox* will open the "Color Picker" dialog box. Here you can choose your color either with the *Eyedropper Tool*, by clicking in the "Foreground Color" box, or by entering the color value manually by choosing the RGB, CMYK, or hex value.

You can select the *Eyedropper Tool* from the *Toolbox* and click to sample a color from any open document.

Alternatively, when you use the *Pencil*, *Brush*, or *Paint Bucket Tool*, you can press the Alt key to access the *Eyedropper Tool* to select a color quickly. You can also select colors and swatches from the "Color Swatches" palettes.

If you are having difficulty making a choice of colors, you can always sample a color swatch from an image you like. Open the image and click *Image>Mode>Indexed Color*. When the "Indexed Color" dialog box appears, use the following settings: *Palette: Local (Perceptual), Colors: 256, Forced: None*. Then click OK.

Now click *Image>Mode> Color Table*. Click to save and name your table— it will be saved as an ACT file. Save it into your *Photoshop/ Presets/Color Swatches* folder so that you can access it at any time.

Saving and Exporting in Different Formats

There are numerous file types with which you can save your work. Here is a quick rundown of some of them.

PSDs

PSD is Photoshop's native file format and it is supported by most digital art programs, including Painter and Sketchbook Pro. It supports multiple layers and effects, which will make files larger. PSDs are a lossless format, which means that you can save repeatedly without harming the image.

JPEGs

JPEGs are the best way of presenting images online or sending via email. The compression is fantastic—file sizes reduce dramatically without too much loss of quality. However, JPEGs do not support layers and the more times you save the same file, the greater the amount of image degradation. It's best to save as a JPEG only when your artwork is finished and no longer requires editing. With JPEGs, you can choose the level of compression you apply to images so that you can control exactly how small the files become. This will affect the image quality, but only by a negligible amount. Photoshop has a "Save for Web" function that results in a very internet-friendly image size with an almost indiscernible loss of quality.

GIFs, PNGs, and TIFFs

A GIF file is limited to 256 colors; it is effective for simple images, but should not be used for anything complex. GIF files can support basic animations suitable for the internet.

A PNG file supports up to 16,000,000 colors and is a lossless format. With PNGs, it is possible to have a transparent background (something unachievable with JPEGs). However, PNGs are often larger than JPEGs so tend to be used less frequently.

A TIFF file is similar to a PSD in that it supports multiple layers and interfaces well with most digital art programs. However, although TIFFs can save adjustment layer preferences for future tweaking, the file sizes are much larger than PSDs.

Which Digital Art Program Is Right For You?

Each of the programs covered here has its own special features for producing digital art effects.

Sketchbook Pro

If you are looking for a program with which you can get started straightaway, then Autodesk Sketchbook Pro is a great choice. It has fewer bells and whistles than other programs so is easy to grasp quite quickly. Many artists start off in Sketchbook Pro, sketching and producing their line work before moving their files over to Photoshop to color and add effects.

Corel Painter

"Designed by artists, for artists," Corel Painter is a highly sophisticated program that produces naturalistic digital artwork with traditional paint effects from watercolors to pastels, oil paints, pencils, and inks.

Painter offers various workspaces tailored to whatever style of painting you desire. As its layout is a lot like Photoshop, it is easy to transfer to Corel Painter if you are familiar with the former program. While Painter doesn't include many of the more advanced Photoshop tricks and layer styles, it is still the best program for traditional paint effects.

Adobe Illustrator

For vector drawings, logo design, typography, and pattern design, you can't beat Adobe Illustrator. However, this program doesn't produce hugely naturalistic work and is not the best at handling textures. It is often used in conjunction with Photoshop to achieve the best results.

Adobe Photoshop

Adobe Photoshop offers the greatest number of options for creating digital art, encompassing all areas from traditional painting to photo retouching. It involves a fairly steep learning curve to begin with, as the interface is far from intuitive, but once you are familiar with this program you will find it extremely versatile.

Chapter Two

Creative Tools

This chapter describes the various creative tools available in digital art programs. It suggests tips and tricks for using them effectively and examines ways in which you can use Photoshop's functions to improve your artwork.

The Pencil Tool and Aliased Pixels

The *Pencil Tool* is probably one of the most misunderstood tools in Photoshop. At first glance, it appears to be a slightly inferior version of the *Brush Tool*. It uses blocky, aliased pixels rather than the smooth, anti-aliased pixels of the brush, but this isn't necessarily a disadvantage.

Crisp lines

Aliased pixels make nice crisp lines which, at high resolution, look remarkably like scanned pencil lines. Aliased pixels also allow you to fill in areas of color precisely and rapidly.

Color fill

Once you have ensured that there are no gaps between your lines drawn with the *Pencil Tool*, switch to the *Paint Bucket Tool* (making sure you uncheck the "Anti-alias" option in the toolbar). Now fill away. If you want to keep your lines on a separate layer, use the *Magic Wand Tool* to select the area to be filled on the "Lines" layer, then move on to your coloring layer and fill in.

Editing colors

Not only is this a speedy method of flat coloring, aliased pixels also allow you to edit colors with minimal hassle.

> **TECHNICAL TIP**
> Don't free transform your lines until you've filled everything with color. Once you have transformed the lines, they will be anti-aliased and won't fill correctly to the edges.

Using aliased pixels allows you to color right to the border so that you can recolor an entire area with one paint-bucket fill.

You can change the mood of your image in minutes. With just the *Paint Bucket Tool* and an orange layer set to *Soft Light*, the illustration has altered significantly.

The Brush Tool

The *Brush Tool* in Photoshop is extremely versatile and will help you achieve an almost limitless number of effects.

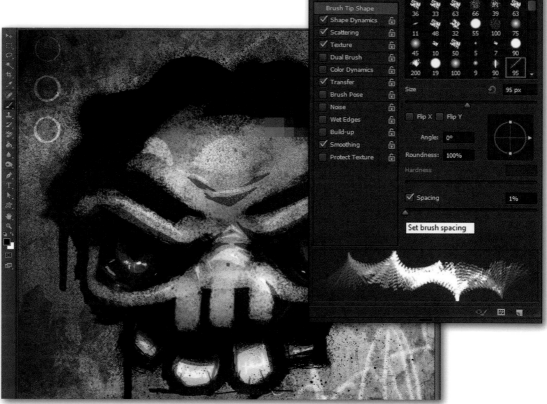

Brush libraries

Photoshop has a range of excellent brush libraries divided into various brush effects. You can choose to use just one set or append multiple sets together. The "Brushes" palette gives you the option to customize brush effects further.

If you set the *Size Jitter* and *Opacity* and *Flow Jitters* to "Pen Pressure," your brush will act intuitively and feel like a real paintbrush. The harder you press down on your stylus, the bigger and bolder your brushstrokes will be. If you can, set the *Angle Jitter* to "Pen Tilt" to make your painting even more authentic.

Increasing or decreasing the spacing of a brush can dramatically change its effect. To see how this works, try looking at the "Brush Preview" window when you click and drag the *Spacing* slider from left to right.

Applying texture to your brushes breaks up the brushstroke and adds a natural grain to your painting.

Enabling the *Dual Brush* will combine two brushes of your choice; this can result in unpredictable outcomes.

Scattering multiplies the number of times that Photoshop will draw the brush-tip shape in a brushstroke. It disperses the shapes along the line you've drawn. You can alter the number and direction of the scatterings.

TECHNICAL TIP
Using the square bracket keys "]" and "[" increases and decreases your brush size. This is much more efficient than changing your preset or dragging the *Size* slider around in the toolbar.

Bristle Brushes and the Mixer Brush

Introduced in Photoshop CS5, bristle brushes have virtual bristles that react to tilt and pressure in a much more advanced way than earlier Photoshop brushes. When you press down with a bristle brush, the bristles splay out on the virtual canvas, just like a real paintbrush, resulting in expressive brushstrokes. Bristle brushes offer much more variety than Photoshop's older, static brushes.

The first stroke in the image above is "low bristles" and "high stiffness"; the second stroke is "low bristles" and "low stiffness"; the third stroke is "high bristles" and "high stiffness"; and the fourth stroke is "high bristles" and "low stiffness."

Bristle qualities

The *Bristles* slider affects the number of bristles in the brush—a high percentage gives a smooth brushstroke, a lower percentage lets you see the individual bristle marks in the artwork.

The *Stiffness* slider alters the rigidity of the brush—a high percentage makes brushstrokes predictable, a lower percentage allows the bristles to move freely, giving expressive strokes.

The preview box at the bottom of the page displays the exact angle at which your brush is tilting, so you can see the position of your brush and the mark it will make on the canvas.

The *Mixer Brush*

The *Mixer Brush* uses the bristle brushes to pick up the digital paint you've already laid down on the canvas and to mix the colors you have on each bristle.

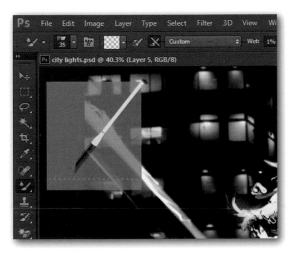

With the "Mix Mode" drop-down menu, you can quickly change the wetness, paint load, and mixing levels without having to tweak each setting. This makes painting feel quick and natural. The best feature about the *Mixer Brush* is its nondestructive painting. You can paint on a separate layer over your artwork because the *Mixer Brush* can sample from all the layers beneath it. This protects the artwork from damage.

The Pen Tool

Photoshop's *Pen Tool* does not work as you might expect. Although its name suggests freehand drawing, the *Pen Tool* is, in fact, used to plot a series of anchor points to create paths with "Bézier" curves.

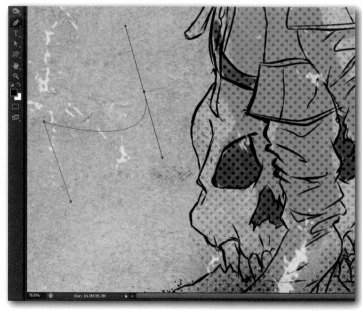

To start a path, click on the canvas with the *Pen Tool*. A second click will create a line between the two anchor points. Click and hold on the second anchor point, then start dragging your cursor to make a Bézier curve.

Using handles

You can make a perfect curve up to a 90° angle. Use the handles that appear after clicking and dragging to control the arc of the curve. Click on an existing anchor point to remove it. To close your path, click on the anchor point with which you began the sequence.

If you have two handles, the curve can be difficult to manipulate. To remove one of the handles, hover the cursor over the anchor point and mouse-click while holding down the Alt key.

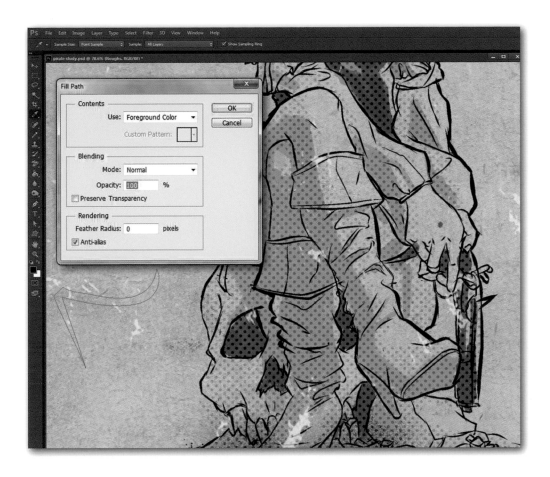

Creating smooth curves

For a smooth effect, place additional anchor points on the path between two curves. Once your path is complete, you can stroke it to create line work or turn it into a selection by right-clicking over the path itself or in the "Paths" palette. The path or selection can then be filled. The path can be accessed at any time in the "Paths" palette, so you only have to draw it once.

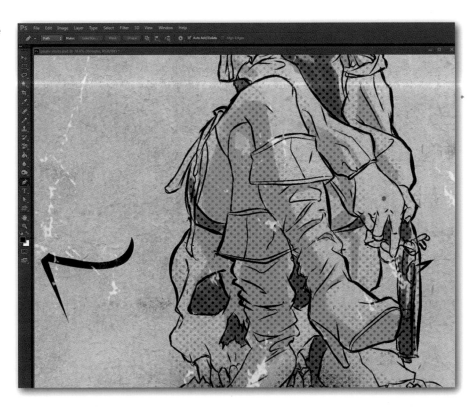

The Eraser Tool

The *Eraser Tool* can be used both for correction and effect.

Eraser modes

The *Eraser Tool* has three modes: "Brush," which gives soft, anti-aliased edges; "Pencil," which makes hard, aliased edges; and "Block," a square brush. You can make the effect subtler by altering the opacity of the eraser in "Pencil" and "Brush" modes. You can also alter the flow in "Brush" mode. The options to alter opacity and flow are not available in "Block" mode. If you want to create subtle, faded edges, use an airbrush eraser set to 50% opacity with "Pen Pressure" enabled.

The *Background Eraser Tool*

The *Background Eraser Tool* removes the background behind complicated foreground elements such as trees. It samples the color at the midpoint of the cursor at the moment of clicking. Then, as you drag the brush across the image, it erases every pixel of the sampled color while leaving other colors untouched.

Moving the cursor over a new color will resample and erase it as well, so be careful how you use this tool. To be on the safe side, set the *Background Eraser Tool* to sample the color once in the *Options Bar*.

If you are erasing similar colors, you can lower the tolerance of the *Background Eraser Tool* so that it only erases specific shades.

The *Background Eraser Tool* is particularly useful if you want to replace a bland-looking sky with a more dramatic one.

The *Magic Eraser Tool*

The *Magic Eraser Tool* removes all colors within a defined tolerance setting. With one click, the surrounding color is erased—there is no need to drag the cursor. The *Magic Eraser Tool* is great for quickly rubbing out large expanses of color.

Soft brush eraser   **Background eraser**

Magic eraser   **Pencil eraser**

The Custom Shape Tool

At first glance, the *Custom Shape Tool* looks as though its only function is to add basic clip art to Photoshop, but there is more to it than meets the eye.

Rectangle Tool	U
Rounded Rectangle Tool	U
Ellipse Tool	U
Polygon Tool	U
Line Tool	U
Custom Shape Tool	U

Making a stamp

The *Custom Shape Tool* works by selecting a predefined symbol and dragging it to make a stamp of it. The stamp can be distorted depending on how you drag the bounding box. Using the *Custom Shape Tool* in this way means that it becomes more like a custom brush tool—it's good for adding random or chaotic detail to images.

W : 15.22 cm
H : 2.54 cm

When you use the *Custom Shape Tool*, you can make an individual shape layer. You can then generate a path from the shape you've just created. Alternatively, you can generate pixels based on the shape you have made.

Each custom shape can be tailored to your needs. It can be filled with a pattern gradient, flat color, or left blank with just a stroked outline.

The image below has been made using the custom shape shown above. By stretching the shape vertically and horizontally, a strong silhouette is created very quickly. First black and then white is used to cut into the shapes to create variety. The mood of the image is further enhanced by the addition of some texture overlays.

Lots of different shapes

When you first access the custom shapes, it may appear that there are only a limited number. However, by clicking on the arrow for the shapes' fly-out menu (located in the *Options Bar*) you can display all the custom shapes available. Suddenly, you'll find you have a lot more to play with! As always, you can edit and create new custom shapes, and many more are available on the internet as free downloads.

The Type Tool

Access the *Type Tool* by pressing T or clicking on the "T" icon in the *Toolbox*. The *Type Tool* creates vectored letters horizontally or vertically, or as type-shaped masks.

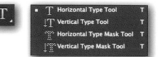

Creating type

You can create type in two ways: either by clicking the mouse at the point where you want to begin and then typing using the keyboard, or by clicking and dragging to select an area where the type will appear in a paragraph. For both options, once you have finished writing your text you need to commit the type to a separate layer by clicking the tick icon.

Transforming

If you want to transform your text, you can use the normal *Free Transformation Tools*. The best way to do this is to click on your paragraph text with the *Type Tool* and drag to resize the handles. The text will automatically reformat to fit the bounding box. To skew the text in your direction of choice, hold down the Cmd and Ctrl keys while you are dragging the handles.

Managing fonts

Fonts are fully editable—you can change their size and color and you can kern (alter the distance between characters). You can "warp" text to a predefined shape or alter the settings manually. You can also type on a path, after first drawing the path with the *Pen Tool,* or by creating a vector shape and then clicking the *Type Tool* on the path.

You can convert type to a fully editable shape by clicking *Layer>Type>Convert to Shape.* This feature is great for designing logos. Once the type has been converted, you can use the *Direct Selection Tool* to manipulate the anchor points of each letter in the same way as you would with the *Pen Tool.*

The Free Transform Mode

Often referred to as the *Free Transform Tool*, this mode allows you to change the size and shape of any element on a layer.

Pressing Ctrl + T creates a bounding box around whatever elements you have on your layer. The box has four corner handles and a reference point in the center. Grab a handle and drag it to alter the shape of the element.

Resizing

If you hold down the Shift key while dragging a handle, you constrain the proportions and maintain the aspect ratio of your element. This allows you to resize it without distorting it. If you hold down the Alt key while dragging the handle, you move the sides of the element an equal distance from the center reference point.

Rotating

If you hover your cursor outside the corner of the bounding box, you can rotate the box's contents. Hover inside the box to move the content.

Rotating the box causes the contents to move around the center reference point. If you want the rotation to be centered on a different point in the box, click and drag the reference points—to a corner, for example. This will form a new axis around which the contents rotate.

Modifying

Right-clicking anywhere within the bounding box allows you to make modifications such as *Skew, Distort, Perspective,* and *Warp.* It also gives you access to simple controls such as *Flip Horizontal* or *Flip Vertical.*

Clicking on *Warp* while using the *Free Transform Tool* will superimpose a grid on the bounding box. You can then warp specific parts of the image by dragging the grid's anchor points.

Blurs

With blurs, you can precisely control the focus of an image. In older versions of Photoshop, one of the most useful blurs is the *Gaussian Blur*, which softens all pixels within a selected area.

◁ The *Motion Blur* simulates movement by controlling the angle and distance of the blur.

▷ The *Radial Blur* can be set to spin or zoom to simulate a dramatic camera effect. All Photoshop's traditional blurs offer a "Preview" window with editable options you can choose from.

The CS6 Blur Gallery

Photoshop CS6 allows you to apply blurs directly to an image with even greater precision; you can also manipulate the blurs in real time!

◁ With *Field Blur*, an image is blurred when you apply pins to it. Pins allow you to control the level of blur surrounding them. You can apply as many pins as you like to an image, so the results are very precise.

▷ The *Iris Blur* brings up an ellipse that you can manipulate to dictate the areas you want to blur. This works well in drawing your attention to items in the center of an image.

◁ The *Tilt-Shift Blur* enables you to replicate tilt-shift photography. You drag the solid lines to delineate the areas you don't want blurred and use the broken lines to indicate where you want the blurs to start

▷ The "Blur Effects" panel in the lower part of the Blur Gallery has content controls to simulate "bokeh" effects. (Bokeh is the way in which a camera blurs and renders out-of-focus points of light.) The *Light Bokeh* slider controls the intensity of the effect, the *Bokeh Color* slider allows you to boost the saturation, and the *Light Range* slider enables you to select the darkest and brightest pixels to be affected.

Filters

There is a tendency for first-time users to deploy filters indiscriminately to create "instant art." A little restraint is the key to using filters.

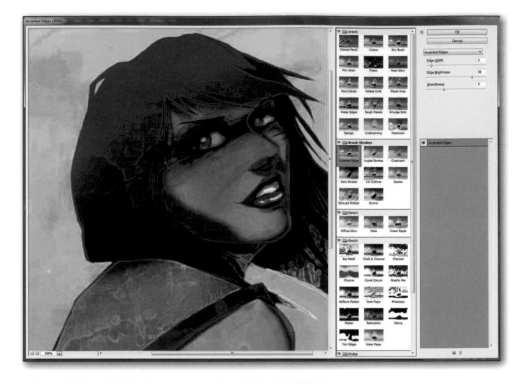

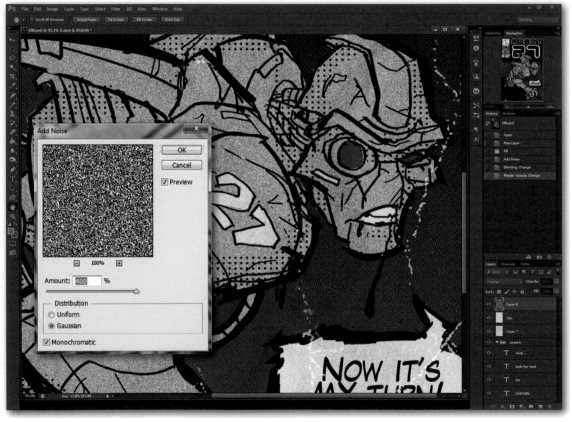

The Filter Gallery

Filters allow you to change the appearance of an image, layer, or selection in a few simple clicks. To access the Filter Gallery, you need to click through the "Filter" menu.

The Filter Gallery is divided into a "Preview" window on the left, a filter selection column in the middle, and a choice of filter options on the right. If you already know which filter you want, you can bypass the Filter Gallery and access your chosen filter directly from the "Filter" menu.

Some of the most useful filters are blur filters and noise filters which add noise and grain to your images. The "Noise" filter can be used to add a layer of detail and prevent banding effects when using gradients. The "Reduce Noise" filter is good for repairing old, damaged photographs.

"Sharpen" filters help to define blurred images by increasing the contrast between pixels.

If a filter isn't working, it's worth checking that you are in RGB mode, as some filters only work in RGB. Also, certain filters are processed entirely in RAM. If you're having problems, try turning off other programs to free up some RAM, and then reopen Photoshop.

You can download numerous high-quality filters from the internet for free.

Layer Masks

Layer masks allow you to hide pixels and bring them back at will. Instead of erasing something permanently, you can apply a layer mask to obscure the area. This gives you more flexibility when working in Photoshop.

You can apply a layer mask by clicking on the circle in the square icon at the bottom of the "Layers" palette. Then use a brush to paint with black to hide pixels (use white to reveal them again). Alternatively, you can use the selection tool of your choice (for example, the *Lasso Tool*) to designate an area in which to apply the layer mask. Using a shade of gray will reduce the opacity of a pixel, making it translucent instead of masking it completely.

Clipping mask layers

The "Clipping Mask" layer acts in the same way as a standard layer mask, but uses the layer beneath as a guide for where pixels should be added. New pixels will only appear over existing pixels beneath; if the area beneath is clear, no new pixels will appear. Clipping mask layers are useful for actions such as applying shading to characters, because they ensure you avoid getting shading on the background as well.

▷ This is what the shading looks like when the clipping masks are released, revealing all the brushwork.

▽ Finished art

Blending Modes

Blending modes affect how layers interact with one another in an image. Blending modes have individual features, but are grouped into similar effects.

The default setting for any new layer is "Normal." Click in the "Layers" palette to change the blending mode of a layer; this will alter the appearance of your image, depending on the layers beneath your active layer.

Contrast boosting effects

This group includes *Overlay*, *Soft Light*, *Hard Light*, *Vivid Light*, *Linear Light*, and *Pin Light*. Each of these modes employs various methods of increasing contrast. The outstanding effects here are *Overlay* and *Soft Light*. *Overlay* multiplies light colors and screens dark colors; *Soft Light* multiplies dark tones and screens light tones. You may find that lowering the opacity when using these modes will help to get the exact look you want.

Darkening effects

This group includes *Darken*, *Multiply*, *Color Burn*, and *Linear Burn*. All these blending modes will make your image significantly darker. *Multiply* is the most reliable mode to choose; it darkens the lower layer in relation to the upper one. White becomes transparent, which is useful for actions such as painting underneath a layer of scanned artwork (the lines remain, but the paper is invisible)

Lightening effects

This group includes *Lighten*, *Screen*, *Color Dodge*, and *Linear Dodge*. All these modes will make your image lighter. *Screen*, the light equivalent of *Multiply*, is the most popular choice; it lightens the lower layer in relation to the upper one.

Component effects

The modes *Hue*, *Saturation*, *Color*, and *Luminosity* all affect an element of their group, while leaving other elements unaffected. For example, *Saturation* lowers the saturation, but does not alter the hue or luminosity.

Use the arrow keys to cycle quickly through the various blending modes to see which work best for your image.

Inversion effects

The modes *Difference* and *Exclusion* react to the differences between the upper and lower layers.

Chapter Three

Creative Concepts

Whether you are working digitally or traditionally, the concepts covered in this chapter offer tips and insights that result in stronger and more effective final artwork.

Composition

Composition, or how you arrange the visual elements in a picture, is vital to its success. There is little point in being able to draw technically if your composition is weak.

It's best to visualize your composition first in thumbnail form, so that you get the overall balance correct before starting to work on the details. If an image is effective at the size of a postage stamp, it will work at the size of a billboard!

Purely symmetrical and balanced compositions (with the main subject positioned centrally in an image) tend to be predictable and dull. Exciting and stimulating images use asymmetry; this is because elements that are off-balance create tension and movement.

Camera angles

It's important to consider the camera angle you use in an image. A close-up shot will lend an air of intimacy and enable the viewer to gauge a character's feelings.

A low-angle shot will increase the viewer's identification with the scene. It will also make the character in an image appear either strong and heroic or domineering and menacing.

A high-angle shot (or bird's-eye view) will make the viewer feel more like a spectator or eavesdropper than someone who is directly involved with the scene. A long shot like this is great for establishing environment and atmosphere, but it doesn't encourage emotional involvement.

Pointers

Strong lines and shapes lead the viewer's eye around the image. Interest is maintained through various "pointers" that guide the eye toward areas of interest. The use of darker, out-of-focus framing elements also draws attention to other areas of interest.

Pointers to main focal point

Pointers to other areas of interest

Reflected and Ambient Light

Reflected light is the light that bounces off the surface of a subject onto surfaces surrounding the subject, and vice versa. Ambient light is a general illumination that comes from all directions and has no visible source.

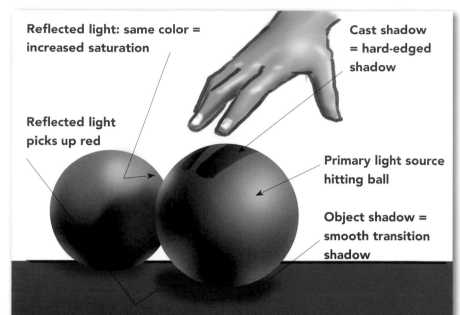

Reflected light: same color = increased saturation

Reflected light picks up red

Cast shadow = hard-edged shadow

Primary light source hitting ball

Object shadow = smooth transition shadow

Reflected light

Reflected light is always located on the subject's shadow side. When light hits a surface, it bounces off it and changes color. If it hits another surface of the same color, the saturation of the color will increase.

In the image below, the primary light source is in front of the gorilla and the secondary light source is behind it. You can see the light bouncing off the gorilla's arms. Light also bounces off the tree trunk and makes it appear green; the surrounding foliage, which is in shadow, appears blue.

Radiosity

Reflected light (known as "radiosity" in 3D computer graphics rendering) helps to unify an image by making everything look like part of a single scene, rather than a collection of disparate elements. Reflected light helps to add depth even to stylized 2D drawings.

Ambient light

Ambient light greatly affects the colors in an image. Consider how the light from an orange sunset makes everything it touches look different. You can replicate ambient light effects by using a photo filter layer in Photoshop. In this image, the ambient light is the cold blue of the forest, which gives all the elements not touched by reflected light a dark blue hue. The light from behind the subject makes the focal points appear to pop forward in the illustration. The color temperature contrast ensures that the gorilla is the first thing to which our eyes are drawn.

◁ Reflected light hits the underside of the gorilla's face, which would otherwise be in total shadow.

Establishing Mood with Color

Careful consideration of your color scheme will benefit your artwork immensely and alter its mood.

Color qualities

Colors have symbolic meanings and can exert a powerful influence over mood. For example, light blue can give a feeling of calm and tranquillity. Dark blue adds an air of mystery and intrigue. Yellow is bright and optimistic, while red often implies excitement or danger. When choosing a color scheme, you can work within your traditional expectations of color or subvert them to achieve an unusual result.

Colors are also associated with temperature. For example, blue and purple will make a scene look cooler, while red and orange will make it warmer. Warm colors appear closer to the viewer, while cool colors make that part of the image recede. Often a combination of warm and cool colors helps you to achieve a feeling of depth in an image.

△ Here the background is colored in purple to add an air of mystery. The character's bright red sash suggests violence and blood. A red tint overlaying the image hints at his dangerous personality.

▷ The same character rendered with a blue-tinted palette. This creates an enigmatic mood, inviting the viewer to guess the character's motivation.

Local color

Another factor to consider is local color. When a light source is strong, it will affect the color of the surrounding elements, tinting everything with its hue. A useful trick is to apply a "Photo Filter" layer in the "Layers" palette; this will give a soft overlaying color to unify all the elements in an image, creating a cohesive scene.

With traditional media, you are committed to your color scheme. One of the best things about working digitally is that you can use Photoshop to add a color layer to test out different moods, without undoing any of the work you have done already.

Drawing Bodies

Although body size and shape are variable, it is worth following certain guidelines to make sure your characters appear in proportion, much as you would when drawing faces.

Anatomically, the average adult human measures between six and eight heads tall, but to create appealing images it is acceptable to aim for the higher end of this scale. Most artists will exaggerate human proportions to at least eight heads tall, as this improves the aesthetic value of the image without making it looking unnatural. Fashion and superhero illustrators tend to use eight-and-a-half heads and nine heads respectively. Men and women are drawn using the same head/height ratios, but women appear shorter as their heads are slightly smaller.

Vertical proportions

For artistic purposes, the typically proportioned adult stands at eight heads tall, with various anatomical details located along the horizontal divisions of each "head."

Horizontal proportions

Although men and women share the same vertical proportions, their horizontal proportions differ considerably. A woman's shoulders are narrower than a man's, but her hips are wider. Stylistically, it is generally more usual to draw men with more angular lines than women.

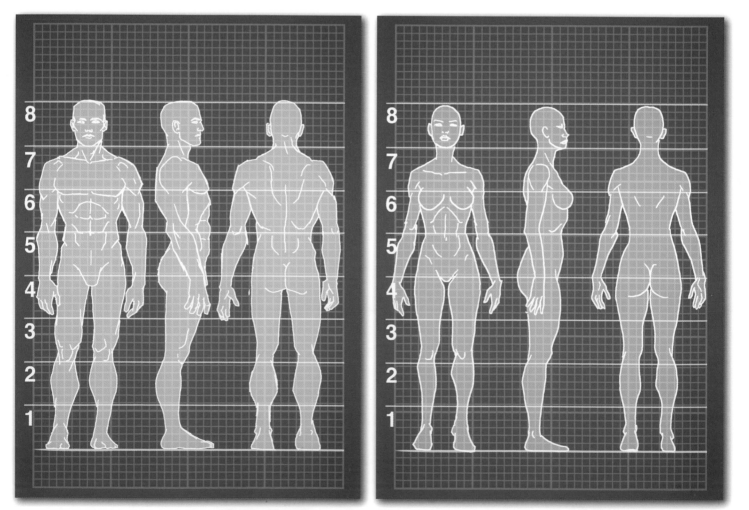

Ideal proportions: male

Ideal proportions: female

Drawing Faces: Proportions

Although we all have different facial features, there are simple guidelines that all faces follow. You can draw these basic head proportions on paper and scan them in when you are ready to develop your drawing, or you can draw your head from scratch on the computer, as I have done here. As soon as you've learned the proportions you'll be able to draw all sorts of characters!

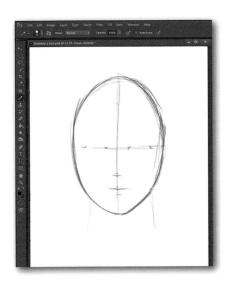

◁ Create a new layer to draw your rough guides. Using a blue-colored brush, start by drawing an oval, then draw a line down the middle. Now make a horizontal line halfway down the oval to create an eye line.

Draw another line halfway between the eye line and the bottom of the oval (the chin) to mark the base of the nose. Finally, draw a line between the nose and the chin that's almost halfway, but slightly closer to the nose.

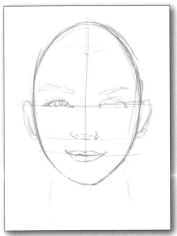

◁ With your guides in place, start to rough out the features, starting with the eyes and mouth. Note that the distance between the eyes should be the width of one eye.

Starting at the eye line, draw the ears by curving slightly upward before drawing downward and finishing on the nose line.

◁ Now the basic proportions of the head are in place, you can develop your character in any way you wish. Add details to suggest personality, such as hairstyle and neck posture. Here I have repositioned the head slightly off center so that the composition is more interesting (remember, asymmetry is always best for composition).

◁ When your roughs are finished, lower the layer's opacity to around 50% and create a new layer.

Use a black brush to draw in the features. Hide your roughs layer when you have finished.

▷ Now you're free to have fun and color in the face!

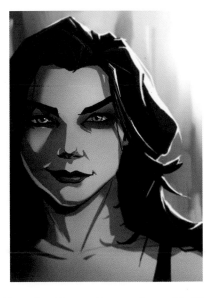

Chapter Four

Digital Art in Action

Now that you understand how Photoshop works and have learned to apply your artistic knowledge, it's time to try some exercises. These will show you how to achieve certain effects and styles digitally and help hone your skills as a digital artist.

Oil Paint Effect

Achieving an oil paint effect in Photoshop is tricky. Although Photoshop CS6 has an oil paint filter and Photoshop CS5 can use the downloadable *Pixel Blender Tool* from Adobe Labs, these options aren't ideal and leave a rather obvious "filter effect." This exercise shows you how to use the "Oil Paint" filter and *Mixer Brush* to create a digital oil painting from a photograph.

Step 1 ▷
Start by selecting your photo. An image showing the sky with clouds will form the basis for a digital artwork inspired by Vincent Van Gogh's famous painting *Starry Night* (above).

◁ **Step 2**
Go to *Filter>Liquify* and select the *Twirl Clockwise Tool* (press C). Click and hold your cursor over the clouds and watch as Photoshop starts to warp them in a spiral. You can even drag the twirling cursor to distort things further. When your clouds are sufficiently stylized, click OK.

Step 3 ▽ ▷

Duplicate the layer by pressing Ctrl + J, then go to *Filter>Oil Paint*. (If you're using an older version of Photoshop, go to *Filter>Pixel Blender>Pixel Blender Gallery* and select "Oil Paint" from the drop-down menu).

The "Oil Paint" filter will produce different results for each photo, so you will have to judge the effects of these sliders by eye. To create a pastiche of *Starry Night*, I've made the *Scale* large and opted for very noticeable effects. We want to be able to see as much detail as possible in the fake brushstrokes.

Step 4 ▷

The canvas weave automatically appears as part of the "Oil Paint" filter. I'm generally happy with how the filter looks, but the effect is a bit strong (everything looks as though it has been run through the "Emboss" filter). To help with this, I've duplicated the original photo layer, dragged it above the filter layer and reduced the opacity to 25%, so that it very slightly masks the embossed quality of the filter layer.

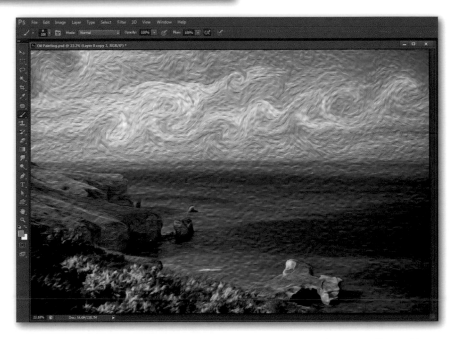

◁ **Step 5**

To paint some extra features into the image, create a layer called "Additions." Use a custom brush of your choice to paint a dark tree in the foreground, making it very curvy and stylized. With the same brush, trace around the edges of the landscape to create outlines; use the darkest local color available for each area. Add some more defined swirls to your sky, if necessary.

Step 6 ▷

Create a new layer called "Mixer Layer." Select the *Mixer Brush* (found in the brush fly-out menu or by pressing Shift + B). Use a *Round Curve* brush (selected from the "Brush" tab) with settings that match the screenshot. Ensure that "clean the brush after each stroke" is unselected in the *Options Bar,* so that the brush continues to pick up paint with each brushstroke you make. Check the "Sample All Layers" box.

▽ **Step 7**

The beauty of using the *Mixer Brush* is that you can paint nondestructively. You can use paint from all the layers, but the brush marks you're putting down will be on a unique layer so that everything underneath it is safe and unharmed.

Apply your paint using fairly large brushstrokes, moving your brush to match the shapes in your photograph. The "Oil Paint" filter has provided a good base image on which to work; if you set the *Mixer Brush* to *1% wet,* it will constantly pick up colors underneath, so all you have to do is move your brush around, thereby effectively cloning paint from the image beneath.

▽ Step 8

Occasionally, you will have to use the *Color Picker* to avoid the paint on your brush interfering with the area you are coloring. In this instance you need to use a blue to paint over the sea, because the white from the clouds would influence the *Mixer Brush*'s strokes too much.

▽ Step 9

For a finishing touch, add a new layer with the blending mode set to *Overlay* to boost the colors of your painting. Use the *Linear Gradient Tool*, set to *Foreground to Transparent, 25% opacity*, to apply some dark blue gradients to the top of the sky. Change to the *Radial Gradient Tool* and use a pale blue color to apply multiple small gradients to the lower portion of the sky. Now pick a highly saturated yellow to apply to the foreground of the image.

Watercolor Cloning in Photoshop CS6

Watercolor cloning allows you to make painterly strokes by sourcing them from an existing photo. For Photoshop CS6, artist Tim Shelbourne and Adobe's Russell Brown have devised an excellent method of watercolor cloning that looks convincing and can be achieved with just a little practice. They have incorporated this into a new Adobe Watercolor Assistant panel that you can download for free from the internet.

This section covers the basic tools supplied with the Watercolor Assistant. However, if you click on the link to the Artists' Quarter (http://theartistsquarterblog.com), in the Watercolor Assistant panel, you can study Tim Shelbourne's more advanced techniques online.

Once you've downloaded and installed the Watercolor Assistant panel, it will take you through the process of constructing your watercolor painting from a photograph. With each step you select, it will run a script that automates various stages of the procedure. This means that you can focus on painting and not worry about getting the layers laid out correctly.

Step 1 ▷

Once you have selected your photo, you'll need to prepare it to get the best result. Go to *Image>Adjustments >Vibrance* and boost the vibrance and saturation levels with the sliders. Make them much higher than you would when editing a photo in the usual way.

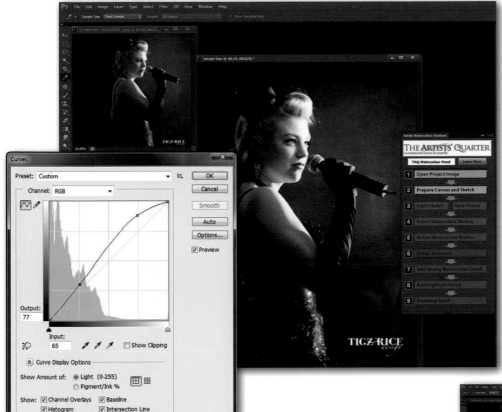

◁ Step 2

Next go to *Image>Adjustments >Curves* and boost the contrast significantly by dragging up on the point shown in the white area of the "Curves" dialog box (as indicated in the screenshot). Move the point in the dark area down slightly.

Step 3 ▷

Now that your photo is prepped, click on Step 2 of the Watercolor Assistant panel. It will prepare your canvas and automatically generate a pencil sketch from your photograph. In Step 3 you can choose between a light or a dark sketch, depending on your needs. The script always creates a light and a dark sketch layer, so if you change your mind later you can just hide or reveal the dark sketch layer in the "Layers" palette.

◁ Step 4

Next click Step 4 in the Watercolor Assistant panel, "Initial Watercolor Washes," to create a clipped vibrance layer (in case you want to edit the vibrance at any point). Then go to the *Pattern Picker* in the *Options Bar* and choose the watercolor pattern of your painting. It will always be the last pattern of the set (the script will have generated it for you automatically).

Step 5 ▷

You will find that you now have the *Pattern Stamp Tool* with a custom brush selected. Use this brush to paint loosely in the first layer. It's important to keep your stylus pressed down as you trace out the colors on the page, as the brush has a multiplying effect and will get darker each time you apply it. The *Pattern Stamp Tool* will have the "Impressionist" option checked; this means you will get a loose interpretation of the colors from the photo beneath, which adds to the watercolor feel.

▽ **Step 6**

When you've finished laying down the first wave of color, switch to the *Smudge Tool*. Using a messy-edged custom brush, smooth out the edges of the paint to make it appear more diffuse, as though it is bleeding out with too much water. It's important to remember that to run the script correctly you must switch back to the *Pattern Stamp Tool* (press S) before moving on to another stage of Watercolor Assistant.

◁ **Step 7**

By clicking on the next stage of Watercolor Assistant you create a new layer and a resized *Pattern Stamp Tool*. You use this for the most important aspect of the image—to build up tone and color. Remember to leave the areas of strong highlights unpainted to reflect the watercolor style. From this stage on, it's important to reference the original photo for the best effect, so either have it open in your workspace or on a separate monitor if you have one.

▽ **Step 8**

When you have finished painting these larger amounts of shading detail, switch to the *Smudge Tool* again to even out some of the paint. Modify the edges to make the paint bleed outside them a little.

Step 9 ▷

Now for the "Detail Recovery" stage, where the brush selected is smaller. It will pick up details from the photo without the "Impressionist" option selected; this makes it more accurate. Paint over the focal points with fairly small strokes. Then smudge these painting strokes so that the lines appear less defined.

◁ **Step 10**

This is the "Strong Watercolor Detail" phase, where the brush you use to clone produces maximum detail, color, and tone. Use it sparingly, and only over the main focal points, or it may damage the watercolor effect.

△ **Step 11**

The final painting stage is the "Add Highlight Detail" section, where the painting layers are merged into one and a layer mask is applied. You're automatically given a texture brush to scratch into the layer mask; this removes the paint and reveals the white paper texture underneath.

△ **Step 12**

Before you move on to the final stage of Watercolor Assistant, go to the light and dark sketch layers and unlock them by clicking on the padlock icon. Press Ctrl + E to merge them down into a single layer, then press B to select a pencil brush and add any lines you need to achieve a more accurate pencil effect.

Once you have finished adding to the lines, reselect the *Smudge Tool* and use it to fade out sections of the lines. This mimics the way in which graphite dissipates through the repeated application of water.

Step 13 ▷

Reopen Watercolor Assistant and click on Stage 9, "Finishing Touch," to apply a high pass layer that will sharpen the details and make your painting look crisp.

Silk-screen Print Effect

Traditional screen printing is great fun, but it is time-consuming to do and expensive to set up. It is much quicker and cheaper to create a screen printing effect in Photoshop.

Step 1 △ ▷

Copy a photo of your choice into a new A4 document. Duplicate your photo by pressing Ctrl + J. Click the small black-and-white circle in the "Layers" palette and select "Threshold" to create a "Threshold" adjustment layer. Adjust the *Threshold Level* slider until you get a result you like.

TECHNICAL TIP
If you can't work out where to make the selection because the threshold result has made it unclear, hide the "Threshold" layer by clicking on the eyeball in the "Layers" palette. Now trace round the subject in the original photo.

◁ **Step 2**

Press Shift + L to access the *Magnetic Lasso Tool* (set it to "Add to Selection" in the options toolbar), and use it to trace round the subject of your photograph.

Step 3 ▷

When your *Magnetic Lasso Tool* selection is complete, press Shift + Ctrl + C to make a copy of the threshold result. Now press Shift + Ctrl + V to paste it into a new layer. Create a new layer underneath the pasted results and fill it with a bright primary color of your choice (in this instance I've used red). Now hide all the other layers.

Step 4 ▷

Add a white stroke border by double-clicking on the pasted layer in the "Layers" palette to open the "Layer Style" dialog box. Click *Stroke* in the left-hand column. Then, in the center column, set *Size, 27 pixels; Position, Outside; Color, white.* Click OK.

◁ **Step 5**

Ctrl-click on the pasted layer's thumbnail in the "Layers" palette to select it. Now go to *Select >Modify >Expand Selection*; expand by 27 pixels and click OK. Double-click on the *Foreground Color Picker* and select a light green color. Then double-click on the *Background Color Picker* to select a dark green color.

Step 6 ▷

Now add a "Gradient Map Adjustment" layer by clicking on the small circle icon in the "Layers" palette. You'll notice that Photoshop has automatically recolored the layer based on the two colors you have picked. If the colors are displayed in the wrong order, simply check the "Reverse" box to switch them round.

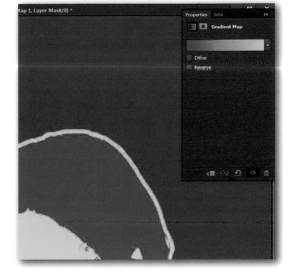

◁ **Step 7**

Click on the "Gradient Map" in the "Layers" palette. Press Shift, click down to the background color layer (selecting the layers you've just been working on) and press Ctrl + G to turn them into a layer group. Name the folder and press Ctrl + J to duplicate it. Rename the new folder "Yellow" and hide the old folder for now.

◁ Step 8

Hide the visibility of the "Gradient Map" in the new layer group and fill the background layer of this group with yellow. Now pick light blue and dark purple as your foreground/background colors and bring back the "Gradient Map" layer. To get the "Gradient Map" to match the new colors you've selected, click on the "Color Gradient" drop-down menu in the "Properties" tab and select "Foreground to Background" (the first swatch in the gallery).

Step 9 ▷

Repeat this process to create two more layer groups, coloring them differently each time. Open a new A4 document. Create two guides dividing the document into quarters by clicking *View>New Guide*. Select *Orientation, Horizontal; Position, 50%*. Follow this procedure again to add a vertical guide.

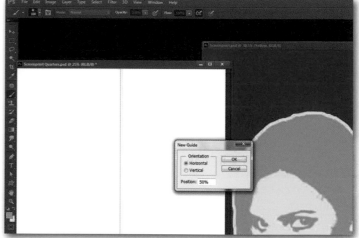

◁ Step 10

In your previous document, press Ctrl + A and Shift + Ctrl + C to copy from all visible layers of one of the layer groups. Paste this into the new document and free transform it (press Ctrl + T) to shrink it down into one of the quadrants. Hold down Shift while transforming to constrain the proportions. You will find that the "Transformation" box will snap to the guides you have created.

Step 11 ▷

When all four color versions of the image are pasted in and shrunk down to size, press Ctrl + H to hide the guides. Now open up and copy an old parchment paper texture and paste it over the images in your new document. Set the blending mode to *Overlay*.

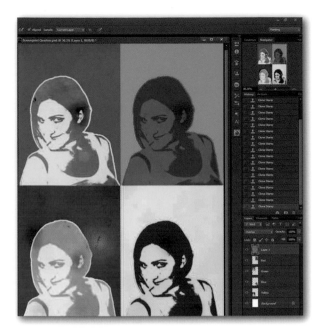

◁ **Step 12**
Press S to select the *Clone Stamp Tool* and use it to clone some interesting bits of texture onto your image. Screen printing often leaves uneven areas of color, so cloning darker areas of texture over your subject will help to simulate this effect. When you have finished, duplicate this texture layer, free transform it, and right-click over the "Transformation" bounding box. Select "Flip Horizontal," click OK, then lower the new layer's opacity to 33% to increase its uneven appearance.

Step 13 ▷

Using the *Square Marquee Tool* (press M), draw a selection over the entire image, then right-click and select "Stroke" from the pop-up menu. Choose *Stroke: Width, 50 pixels; Color, white; Location, Inside.* Click OK to create a white border round the image.

◁ **Step 14**
Make a new layer and press Ctrl + H to reveal the guides again. Select a hard-edged brush (press B) and set it to 50 pixels. Move your cursor to where the guides intersect. Press your stylus onto the canvas and hold down Shift to draw lines vertically. The brush will snap to the guides. Pressing Shift will ensure you continue to draw in a straight line. Repeat this action to draw the horizontal lines. If necessary, nudge your images up to fit the new border. Do this by pressing V to access the *Move Tool* and using the "Up" arrow key to move each layer into position.

Highlights, Glows, and Shadows

One of the advantages of digital over traditional art is that it allows you to create effects like highlights and glows with minimal effort. You can also produce shadow layers, where changing the base colors allows for great versatility.

◁ Step 1

After laying out your base colors for the image, create a new "Clipping Mask" layer and set the blending mode to *Linear Burn* at 65% opacity. (The *Linear Burn* blending mode allows more color to show through than the *Multiply* blending mode, which darkens colors that are applied to the layer.) You can use whatever color you like to apply shading to this layer, but I would recommend *R:137, G:118, B:118*, as this combination works well with any color underneath it.

Step 2 ▷

My preference is for cel shading (the name harks back to an era when cartoons were drawn on animation cels). I use a hard-edged brush or the *Pencil Tool*, alongside the *Lasso Tool*, to apply shading. But any type of shading will work well on the "Linear Burn" layer. If you prefer a softer style of shading, you can use the *Linear* and *Radial Gradient Tools* and an airbrush. You can create a nice effect by combining these two styles of shading.

△ Step 3

Another approach to shading is to make your base colors darker and apply highlights to your work. This means you won't have to add highlights at a later stage. Create an *Overlay* layer over your base colors and line work and use pure white to add highlights; this will brighten the colors beneath.

△ ▷ Step 4

Highlights always look more convincing when the light bleeds out slightly from the edge of the shadows, much as it does in real life. Fortunately, Photoshop allows you to select *Luminosity* (the bright parts of an image) with one simple action: Ctrl + Alt + 2. Press Shift + Ctrl + C, followed by Shift + Ctrl + V, to paste in a copy of the light parts of this image. Now change the blending mode to *Overlay* and apply a *Gaussian Blur* to make the light scatter slightly over the shadows.

◁ Step 5

When an object glows, the center is pure white. It's only as the glow scatters from the center that we notice any color. Draw the elements you want to glow in pure white and on their own layer. Then create a layer underneath and set its blending mode to *Screen*, so that any light you render on the layer will be translucent. Select the *Radial Gradient Tool,* setting "Foreground to Transparent" and 25% opacity, and choose a highly saturated version of the color you want for the glow. Drag the *Gradient Tool* outward from the white center and you will instantly have your simulated glow.

Step 6 ▷

To add a more opaque glow (particularly effective for rim lighting) create a layer set to *Linear Dodge* mode and apply your lighting with a low saturation version of the glow color. For example, use a soft pink to reflect a red light.

▽ Step 7

To make the light effects more intense, simply double up on the "Linear Dodge" layers to show various levels of light.

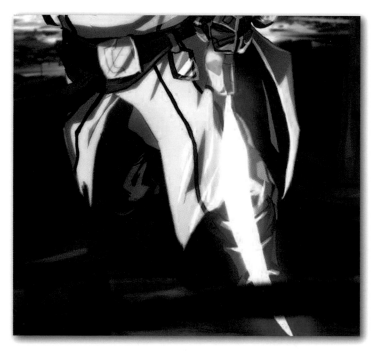

Step 8 ▷

One way to make your shadows look richer is to create a "Clipping Mask" layer immediately over your base colors and beneath your "Shading/Highlight" layers. Apply tints of color with the *Radial Gradient Tool*, using warmer tones for foreground elements and cooler shades for the background.

Step 9

To create smaller particle glows, use a white color speckle brush to paint in the center of your particle lights. Double-click on the layer in the "Layers" palette to bring up the "Layer Style" menu. In the left-hand column, click on *Outer Glow* to access its options. In the center panel, set as follows: *Blend Mode, Color Dodge; Opacity, 75%*. Choose an appropriate color for your glow. Anything you paint on this layer will now automatically have a glow around it.

Step 10

One of the advantages of using a "Color Dodge" layer for multiple glows is that you can edit it at any time. As you've applied a layer style, you can instantly effect changes to everything on the layer. For example, if you want to change the color, intensity, or distribution of the glows, just double-click on the layer and edit the options from the "Layer Style" dialog box. Here, by switching the color in the layer style to yellow and adjusting the hue (via *Hue/Saturation*) of the "Glow" layer below, I've changed the pirate's energy sword from red to yellow in just a few clicks.

Step 11

When you've finished rendering the rest of your image, add an "Overlay" layer and use the *Radial Gradient Tool* to add various soft glows to tint the environment and the character. For example, add a hint of red to the pirate's face, illuminate his shoulder pad, and bring the glows out further from the aurora borealis effect in the background to make them more colorful and dramatic.

Drawing from Reference

For this exercise, I was inspired by a photograph of my daughter rummaging among my things and I used the picture as a starting point for my digital art. Ignore the detractors—any artist worth their salt will tell you the value of drawing from reference. The key is not to be a slave to it, but to be inspired by it.

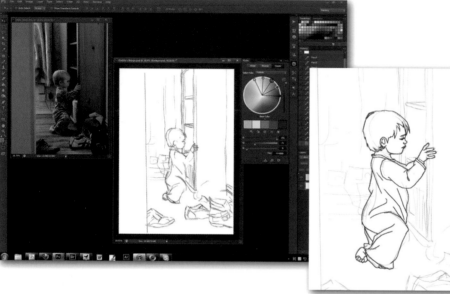

◁ **Step 1**

Open up your reference photo alongside your new image. Use a light blue brush to draw in your roughs based on the photograph. Lower the opacity of the layer to around 45%. Create a new layer called "Lines" and use a black brush to draw your finished line work.

Step 2 ▷

Hide the "Roughs" layer by clicking on the eyeball icon in the "Layers" palette. Press Ctrl + J to duplicate the "Lines" layer and name this new layer "Flats." Press G to select the *Paint Bucket Tool* and use it to fill in the areas of flat color. Don't feel you have to be restricted by the colors in your photograph: it's often much better to choose new colors to suit the mood of your illustration.

◁ **Step 3**

Create a new layer, set it to *Overlay* and name it "Highlights." Use the *Pencil Tool* with a pure white color to render the highlights on the child, the curtain, the shelves, and the shoes. Switch to a soft airbrush with the same white color to paint in the highlights on the walls and floor.

◁ Step 4

I decided to change the color of the lines from black to red to make them fit better with the overall color scheme of the picture. To do this, lock the transparent pixels on the "Lines" layer by clicking on the small chessboard icon in the "Layers" palette. Press Shift + Backspace and select "Use Foreground Color" to fill the lines with a dark red.

△ Step 5

Create a new layer called "Color Tints." Use the *Magic Wand Tool* (press W) to select an area on the "Flats" layer, then switch to the "Color Tints" layer. Select the *Linear Gradient Tool* (press Shift + G) and use a variety of lighter and darker colors to apply some smooth shading to the image.

Step 6 ▷

Time to add a paint texture. Choose an existing photo of a paint texture (there are numerous free textures online). Open the paint texture file and go to *Image>Adjust>Hue/Saturation*. Move the *Saturation* slider all the way to the left to desaturate the image. Copy and paste the paint texture on top of your artwork and set the "Layers" blending mode to *Overlay*.

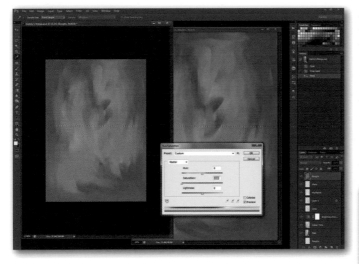

Step 7 ▷

Create a new layer set to *Linear Dodge* and make a selection of the highlights by Ctrl-clicking on them. Then use a light yellow color to paint in and boost the highlights on the new layer. To simulate the way in which light scatters and to boost the richness of the light, press Ctrl + Alt + 2. This makes a selection of the *Luminosity* (all the light areas of the image). Press Shift + Ctrl + C, then Shift + Ctrl + V to paste a merged version of the light areas over your artwork. Set the layer to *Overlay*. Click on *Filter>Blur>Gaussian Blur* and use a blur of around 7 pixels.

In the final image (page 60, top right) you can see how the added patterns and textures combine with the blended highlights to create a warm, homely composition.

◁ Step 8

As a finishing touch, introduce a patterned effect to the curtains. Use the *Magic Wand Tool* to select the curtains and paste a patterned texture into the area. Choose *Edit>Paste Into* and change the blending mode to *Soft Light* at 79% opacity.

Glossary

Bezier curves: A parametric curve frequently used in graphics.

Bitmap: A rasterized graphic image made up of a rectangular grid of pixels in which the pixel is either black or white. Most images on computers are bitmap images.

CMYK: The four inks used in process-color printing (cyan, magenta, yellow, and key/black). Also known as subtractive color.

Composition: The arrangement of the visual elements in a picture.

DPI: Dots per inch. A measurement of dot density in printing or video.

GIF (Graphic Interchange Format): A file that is limited to 256 colors and is effective for simple images.

Grayscale: An image with no color hues, but a range of gray levels as opposed to simply black and white. Grayscale images are measured as percentages of black ink coverage (0% is equal to white and 100% equal to black).

Hex values: (also called hexadecimal color values) These comprise of a six-digit alphanumeric combination that represents a specific color.

Hierarchy: Visual hierarchy in an image is the organization of content with the emphasis on particular elements. The largest objects are not necessarily the focus of interest.

Hue: A color or shade.

JPEG (Joint Photographic Experts Group): A standardized image compression format used for compressing full color or grayscale images.

Layer: Layers are key features in graphics programs. They allow the artist to separate parts of an artwork digitally, and to edit or delete one of the layers without impacting on other layers. An adjustment layer allows nondestructive color changes to layers beneath it.

Layer mask: Linked to a layer, the mask hides part of the layer from the image, thereby controlling what is visible. Layer masking allows you to hide or use as much of the layer as you wish.

Lossless: This type of compression reduces the size of a file without loss of quality.

Native resolution: The resolution at which a television screen or monitor is designed to display images; its single fixed resolution. The native resolution of a computer screen is 72 DPI.

Pixel: The word is a combination of "picture" and "element." In digital imaging, a pixel (or pel) is the smallest controllable element in a display device, the smallest representative component of a raster image.

Pixelate: To cause an image to break into visible pixels by enlarging it too much.

PNG (Portable Network Graphics): A file format for storage of digital images. It supports up to 16,0000,000 colors and is a lossless format.

PPI (Pixels per inch): A measurement of the resolution or density of pixels in digital images on various devices (computer monitors, digital camera sensors, etc.).

PSD (Photoshop Document): Photoshop's native file format, supporting multiple layers and effects.

Radiosity: Reflected light in 3D computer graphics rendering.

Ram (or Random Access Memory): Computer data storage system in which data can be retrieved in any order.

Raster image: An image defined as a collection of pixels arranged in a rectangular array of lines of dots or pixels.

RGB: An additive color model in which red, green, and blue light are combined to produce colors; generally for monitors, TV screens, and digital cameras.

TIFF (Tagged Image Format File): A file format for digital images. It supports multiple layers and interfaces well with most digital art programs.

Vectors: Lines, curves, objects, and shapes, calculated mathematically to represent images.

Further Reading

Addison, Martin. *Painter 12 for Photographers*. Focal Press, 2011.

Aleksander, Nykolai. *Beginner's Guide to Digital Painting in Photoshop*. 3DTotal Publishing, 2012.

Beccia, Carlyn. *Digital Painting for the Complete Beginner*. Watson Guptill, 2012.

Caplin, Steve. *How to Cheat in Photoshop CS6: The Art of Creating Realistic Photomontages*. Focal Press, 2012.

Draws, Rhoda Grossman. *Digital Painting Fundamentals with Corel Painter 12*. Course Technology PTR/ Cengage Learning, 2011.

Ligon, Scott. *Digital Art Revolution: Creating Fine Art with Photoshop*. Watson Guptill, 2010.

Ruppel, Robh. *Digital Painting Techniques* (Volume 3). 3DTotal Publishing, 2011.

Sullins, Angi and Toball, Silas. *Digital Art Wonderland (Creative Techniques for Inspirational Journaling and Beautiful Blogging)*. Northlight Books, 2011.

Tonge, Gary. *A Digital Painting Bible*. Impact, 2008.

Tonge, Gary. *Digital Painting Techniques: Practical Techniques of Digital Art Masters*. Focal Press, 2009.

Tonge, Gary. *Digital Painting Tricks & Techniques: 100 Ways to Improve Your CG Art*. Impact, 2011.

Tuttle, Susan. *Digital Expressions: Creating Digital Art with Adobe Photoshop Elements*. Northlight Books, 2010.

Valentine, Scott. *The Hidden Power of Blend Modes in Adobe Photoshop*. Adobe Press, 2012.